The Grand Experiment

What would happen if a local foundation were to provide select nonprofits with access to fundraising counsel?

Melvin B. Shaw, M.A. Ed.
Pearl D. Shaw, M.P.A, C.F.R.E.

Copyright © 2015 Melvin B. Shaw and Pearl D. Shaw

All rights reserved. No part of this book may be reproduced or transmitted in any form or by any means, electronic or mechanical, including photocopying, recording or by an information storage and retrieval system, without permission in writing from the publisher.

First printing – January 2015
Printed in the United States of America

This book is dedicated to Dr. Jan Young, executive director of The Assisi Foundation of Memphis, Inc. We admire her intuition, vision, and leadership. We appreciate her creativity and willingness to experiment. We also dedicate this book to those organizations who participated in the first round of this "grand experiment." We truly enjoyed our work with each of you and look forward to supporting your continued success.

Special thanks to Sara Henneberger and Jill Keith for their work in bringing this book to life.

Table of Contents

Preface i

Executive Summary ii

Introduction iii

The Grand Experiment 1

Impact To Date 5

"Aha" Moments 6-8

Rationale For counselOnDEMAND 9

Overview of Work With Participating Organizations 11

Case For Support - Economic Development & Urban Farming Grassroots Org. 12

Not The Right Time - School-Based Tutoring Program 13

Board Involvement Established - Performing Arts Organization 14-15

Case For Support - Community Development Intermediary 16-17

Building A Fundraising Program - Health Center 18

Strategy Development And Case - Community Theatre 19

Reflections 20-22

Growing The Grand Experiment 23

Prerequisites Assessment 24

About counselOnDEMAND 25

About Saad&Shaw 26

Meet the Authors 27

Preface

Frequently we receive requests for technical assistance, capacity building, fundraising support, and salaries for development directors. These requests come from a variety of groups at different stages of organizational evolution. Many think money is THE answer to whatever may be going on with their organization. The challenges facing these organizations (large and small; emerging or established), though varied and diverse, often share familiar themes. In some cases, we engage with organizations that thought they wanted or needed one type of assistance, when they actually wanted or needed something else.

We decided to explore the most effective ways to support the organizations we serve in our community. During a brainstorming session, we looked at a micro-consulting program offered by Saad&Shaw. Because we had worked with this fund development firm in the past, we were familiar with their style and results. Their counselOnDEMAND offered several attractive elements, including opportunities to:

- Contract for a finite number of hours;
- Gain insight into what each organization thinks is most important to address during an initial block of consulting time;
- Observe what each organization would do with, during, and after the initial block of consulting hours; and
- Explore differences among type, size, chronological age, and stage of evolution of the organizations served.

We decided to invite select organizations to accept a non-monetary technical assistance grant, and we connected them with Saad&Shaw. We made payments to Saad&Shaw for blocks of consulting time, which we allocated to each participating organization.

Working within a specific block of time (ranging from five to 20 hours) seemed to help most of the organizations more quickly focus on their priorities OR determine their level of readiness for a major fundraising effort, strategic business plan, or project. As a funder, we were able to direct resources to a greater pool of grantees, with sometimes better results than if we had made a single grant of a similar amount to one organization.

Communication, in some cases, improved between us as the funder and the grantee organizations. It is too early in this "grand experiment" to look at all we can learn from the experiences of the organizations served, but the overall feedback has been positive to date.

Dr. Jan Young
Executive Director
The Assisi Foundation of Memphis, Inc.

Executive Summary

Fundraising capacity and infrastructure are the foundation of nonprofit sustainability. Yet many nonprofits struggle to build and sustain these. When seeking to grow their revenue, nonprofits often look to increase their professional fundraising staff. Sometimes these investments pay off handsomely. Other times a revolving door evolves, with staff joining and leaving for many reasons, without a change in fundraising results.

Our experience has shown that small investments in fundraising counsel can help nonprofit leaders increase their knowledge and understanding of fundraising, and begin to implement appropriate strategies. These investments can help ensure that future larger investments are appropriately managed, and at times can uncover previously unrecognized talents and alternatives.

In 2014, The Assisi Foundation of Memphis, Inc., under the direction of executive director Dr. Jan Young, launched The Grand Experiment with Saad&Shaw to learn how nonprofits would respond to the opportunity to work with fundraising counsel. She awarded non-monetary technical assistance grants in amounts ranging from five to twenty hours to six mid-South nonprofits.

> The selected nonprofits included those with a culture and history of successful fundraising as well as emerging grassroots organizations. The results were impressive.
> - Over $1.5 million in grants and in-kind resources from foundations, granting agencies, or individuals has been raised/pledged to date.
> - One organization produced a case for support brochure and secured funding for a small-scale feasibility study and fundraising plan.
> - One moved from planning a staff-led campaign to launching a board-led campaign with staff support.
> - One secured the majority of equipment it needed for expansion through in-kind resources.
> - One realized it was unwilling to make the changes required to diversify funding and expand operations.
> - One wants to continue working with Saad&Shaw, requesting a fundraising plan and ongoing counselOnDEMAND services to build fundraising capacity beyond the executive director.
> - All reported they gained new insights into fundraising, fund development, and donor cultivation, solicitation, retention, and engagement.

Introduction

Can five, 10, or 20 hours of fundraising counsel make a difference in the life of a mid-South nonprofit? One foundation executive launched The Grand Experiment to measure the potential impact.

This report documents our experiences working with The Assisi Foundation of Memphis, Inc. and six mid-South nonprofit organizations during 2014. We share with you the process, near-term outcomes, "Aha!" moments from within the nonprofits, and our reflections.

We documented this work in the hopes that foundation executives and trustees would consider bringing such a service to their grantees. The non-monetary technical assistance grants made by The Assisi Foundation provided local nonprofits with a unique opportunity. And — as you will read — each organization took full advantage of the offer.

We also documented this work so that nonprofit organizations and institutions could learn what others were able to accomplish with the help of a small amount of counsel.

This work was initiated by Dr. Jan Young, the executive director of The Assisi Foundation. We cannot offer enough praise of her leadership. An experienced, talented, and intuitive leader, she took a risk, and the impact has been far-reaching. To date, the 90 hours of fundraising counsel she purchased have resulted in more than $1.5 million in grants and in-kind resources from foundations, granting agencies, or individuals.

It truly has been a "grand experiment."

Thank you for taking the time to read.

Mel and Pearl Shaw

Saad&Shaw's counselOnDEMAND provides flexible, low-cost fund development coaching and strategy sessions for nonprofit executives and development directors. Through this service we help nonprofits meet their fundraising challenges and optimize their resources and staff. Nonprofits receive five hours of counsel in person or by phone and email each month for one to three months. Conversations can be one-on-one with an executive or include staff and board members.

The Grand Experiment

True to its name, The Grand Experiment was just that — an experiment. Dr. Jan Young, the executive director of the Assisi Foundation of Memphis, Inc., – a mid-South foundation – gave selected nonprofits the opportunity to work with fundraising counsel, no strings attached. Dr. Young awarded five-hour blocks of time to nonprofits of her choosing. The process began with an email award notice introducing Saad&Shaw, and letting the nonprofit know how much time had been allotted for us to work together. Emails were typically short and informal.

Once received, we would reach out to the nonprofit and introduce ourselves. We began each engagement with an in-person meeting designed to uncover what the organization would like to achieve during our work together. We typically came prepared with a suggested agenda to guide the first session, with the majority of the time allocated to listening.

> *"Mel and Pearl,*
> *Meet Mike and Karen.*
> *Please provide three blocks of CounselonDEMAND*
> *Many thanks."*

Our initial meetings typically lasted one hour, although one lasted almost two hours. Many used the time to share the history of their organization in general, and their history (or lack of history) specifically with fundraising. Most shared their challenges, though two focused on the opportunities they wanted to take advantage of.

During our first meeting we also provided each organization with a copy of our book *Prerequisites for Fundraising Success*. Some also received a copy of *The Fundraisers' Guide to Soliciting Gifts*. We encouraged those participating in our sessions to read the books and to refer to them as an additional form of technical assistance.

The majority of our work during The Grand Experiment was conducted in person, with follow-up work completed and shared electronically or by phone. All sessions were with the executive director, though one engagement began with the development director. Three of the six organizations had a development director; three had no staff dedicated solely to development. Four of the participating organizations had never before worked one-on-one with professional fundraising counsel; two organizations had prior experience. Of those two, one had received assistance in the identification of capital funders and the writing of proposals but did not have access to counsel that included board and volunteer engagement or the engagement of individual donors.

Much of our time was dedicated to listening to people's visions, challenges, plans, and perceived limitations. We also asked questions:

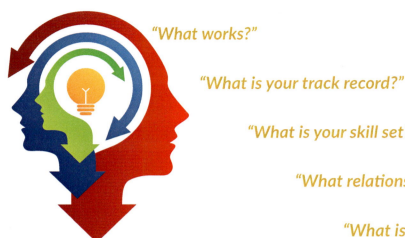

"What works?"

"What is your track record?"

"What is your skill set?"

"What relationships are in place?"

"What is the role of your board?"

And, we challenged assumptions regarding who would give and lead, and why (or why not).

Five of the six organizations experienced meaningful impacts from this counsel; one will begin work in January 2015. Two of the nonprofits chose to use the time to create a case for support and four requested guidance and coaching related to the launch of a proposed annual or major gifts campaign.

The majority of time was used for:

1. Coaching and strategy sessions conducted by phone and in person.

These included conversations related to the differences between volunteer-led fundraising and staff-led fundraising; identification of internal challenges that could be perceived as a barrier to increased investment and growth; how and why individuals become involved as fundraising volunteers; the role of the case for support; the level of preparation required for successful fundraising; the importance of trusting board members to take ownership and leadership; and the importance of building diverse revenue streams before funding from a primary source appears to be in jeopardy.

Conversations also focused on long-term strategy development, potential staffing configurations, and prep for a foundation presentation.

2. Creation of "suggested next steps" and "homework" documents to guide work between meetings and/or after our engagement.

After many of the meetings we created follow-up assignments for the executive and his/her team to complete.

The purpose of this was to keep the organization engaged and to help ensure that other competing priorities would not inhibit a focus on fundraising. Additionally, as counsel our role is to facilitate learning and action on the part of the organization.

"Homework" is a tool designed to keep the organization focused on fundraising related activities in between sessions, to create accountability, and to generate a sense of urgency. Our experience has shown that fundraising-related activities must become a part of an organization's daily work if it is to build and sustain a culture of fundraising.

Too often fundraising is perceived as "asking for money" — an activity that is put off as long as possible. Expanding the definition to include the many activities related to fundraising preparation — and integrating those tasks into the ongoing work of the organization — is an important first step that is often overlooked.

Finally, part of our time was allocated to reviewing and critiquing "homework" and creating additional "suggested next steps" after such reviews.

3. Guidance, direction, editing, and writing of the case for support.

Two organizations decided at the beginning of their engagement that they wanted to create a case for support. One decided later that this would be an important next step and requested additional time to focus on the case.

The process of creating the case is an activity that forces an organization to examine, recommit to, or refine the very fundamentals of its existence.

> We also ask each to compile statistics, quotes, financial information, demographics and images for inclusion in the final piece. Initial drafts were then subject to the "poke test." This is the process of "poking" at the numbers and statements to learn what is behind them, and the extent to which they are accurate and tie to the organization's mission, vision and strategic plan.

Each organization was asked to define its mission, vision, and goals for the next three years, and current as well as projected impact. Most importantly we quizzed leadership on their ability to deliver on their vision, what it would actually cost, and what the projected impact would be.

For one organization, the process of creating the case for support informed the process of updating its business plan, which was going on simultaneously. For the two organizations that completed their case, the process helped pull together in one document their many successes.

Prior to creating the case neither had a full snapshot of the extent of their success.

4. Design and facilitation of board workshops including role playing scenarios, quizzes, and group exercises.

One organization chose to use the time for board engagement. They asked us to facilitate two 90-minute workshops. What they didn't know was the amount of time we allocate to preparing for workshops and following up afterward.

What began as a five-hour engagement turned into a 15-hour one with tremendous results: the board took ownership of the fundraising process. We prepared custom content for the two requested workshops, with the majority of time allocated for small group work and discussion.

Exercises were developed to encourage board members to take initiative in refining the case for support (first workshop), and in role-playing gift solicitation meetings (second workshop).

Impact To Date

Since receiving counsel from Saad&Shaw, participating organizations have experienced a variety of successes.

The economic development and urban farming grassroots organization secured $64,300 in cash and in-kind resources, including $3,000 from a crowd-sourced fundraising campaign, $4,800 in cash funding, and a $39,500 state grant. The in-kind resources were for the major items needed to expand operations, including a walk-in cooler freezer ($12,000 value), supplies for an aquaponics project, bees, and chickens.

The established performing arts organization raised $1,340,000 in less than six months. This board-led campaign secured $700,000 in gifts and pledges from campaign committee members and board members, and a $640,000 matching grant from a local foundation.

The community theatre secured a two-year $150,000 grant to cover staffing and other costs related to the launch of an enhanced annual campaign that targets donors who gave to its recent capital campaign, as well as season ticket holders.

The community development intermediary secured $30,000 to pay for feasibility interviews and a multi-year campaign plan. The interviews are complete and creation of the campaign plan is in process.

The school-based tutoring program gained a deeper understanding of the data and information they would need to collect and communicate in order to engage target donors for expanded operations.

The health center committed to integrating ongoing fundraising into its operations, and to exploring the possibility of establishing a foundation to raise funds for the clinic. Further work will commence in January 2015.

"Aha" Moments

The following are examples of feedback we received from participating nonprofit organizations.

> You showed us that we should make things two-way — it's not just about needing money. You showed us that we should ask for ongoing support beyond getting into the new building.

> Having listened to what direction we wanted to go, you guys put it in a concise manner so we could stay on track.

> It has broadened my idea of what fundraising and development is. Before this I had a very limited scope of what fundraising is: going up to a person and asking them for a donation. I have learned about more possibilities.

> Having such guidance is absolutely necessary for us to make the leap from good to great.

> I received encouragement to give board members independence as fundraisers on their own, instead of carrying the weight as the only fundraising professional.

> By this time next year we will be on our way to becoming self-sustaining.

> One of my most critical roles as a CEO is fund developer. This increased knowledge of processes of fundraising that I didn't have initially.

> It impacted us greatly in terms of us being educated to the fundraising process, which I personally was new to and didn't have a lot of experience in. Just talking with you guys about process has been very helpful to me and has been passed onto the organization and the board.

"Aha" Moments *continued*

> The changing of a mind-set and a culture and a system has to happen before the powers that be will be receptive to the changes that need to happen for us to become a national organization. We have to have systemic changes for that to happen. But they want to keep things the way they are.

> It is mind-blowing the position we are in right now.

> The difference in income is hysterical. Last year we could count the money, this year we have to try and count the money. We are playing catch-up! Everything is going so fast, we are amazed.

> The case for support you shared with us is an example of what we need to do.

> We have to be able to tell a story that our target donors can understand.

> People are giving at such high levels ... our prior campaign had a very low level of board giving. Most were giving $1,500 per year. Now it is $10,000 annually, with campaign giving over and above annual giving. This level of giving only comes when people are surrounded by a group of equally committed individuals. This happens because of the conversations you started.

> We also helped another organization get money through a city program. They got $2,500.

> It was helpful to put the numbers in terms that were real versus making the numbers small. We had to realize that the director's time and work is worth more than he was estimating in the past. You emphasized this regularly and it made a difference.

continued "Aha" Moments

> We need to focus in more. There are so many things in the course of the day that pull us away from fundraising, but it is a crucial part of our operation and we need to treat it as such.

> We know what we need to do, but we are stuck in a hard place to do it.

> Wouldn't have formed in the way it did in a healthy, organic, high-investment way without your encouragement and advisement. One hundred percent of the six-member campaign committee have made leadership pledges in addition to their annual commitments.

> Work with Saad&Shaw was a catalyst for the board to take ownership.

> You guys are aware of what it is like to be in the position that I am in and the unorthodox position I am in, in terms of the board. Meeting with you helped me to change my approach and not let things bother me so much. You helped me take the attitude, 'It is what it is.'

> You have set us on the right course. You showed us that we were just a few steps from victory. I really truly liked the comfort level that you provide ... when people give me elongated words that I have to look up in the dictionary, they lose me."

> You try to give people a very hard look at themselves, and that is very difficult.

> We used language from the Saad&Shaw package to request funds.

Rationale For counselOnDEMAND

We created counselOnDEMAND as a way to provide nonprofit organizations and institutions with access to low cost, high quality fundraising counsel when they need it. counselOnDEMAND gives nonprofits the opportunity to purchase small amounts of fundraising expertise.

It makes access to fundraising counsel affordable.

In many instances, organizations and institutions engage counsel as they are preparing for a major fundraising campaign. This is typically a large investment of time and resources that is expected to result in fundraising that transforms an organization or helps it grow to a new level.

Rationale For counselOnDEMAND

What is less available is access to counsel outside of large campaigns.

Organizations are reluctant to allocate funds for coaching or counsel, and there is limited access to capacity-building funds. The result is organizations with limited knowledge of fundraising who are dependent on foundation grants and revenue from special events.

counselOnDEMAND is designed, in part, to address these challenges. Described as an "intervention" by Dr. Young, counselOnDEMAND creates a space for nonprofit leaders to assess their fundraising readiness and capacity, and most importantly to focus on "unleveraged assets."

Our experience has shown that many nonprofits focus on "hiring a development director" before looking at the relationships and resources that they have access to but have not yet leveraged.

These assets vary from organization to organizations. A common asset is the board. Changing the relationship with individual board members, and the dynamics between staff and board is a process that can be transformational. It can begin with asking questions, allocating time and creating a true partnership.

counselOnDEMAND is a service that helps nonprofits gain an understanding of the prerequisites for fundraising success. It is designed to help organizations build their fundraising capacity and infrastructure long before the launch of a major campaign. We have documented the prerequisites for fundraising success in our book of the same name, and use that book as part of our "curriculum" when working with nonprofits large and small.

We have learned that it is important for organizations to have access to personal, one-on-one conversations with counsel, and to have written tools that supplement those conversations. The written component of our work helps to ensure that the purchase (or technical assistance grant) of "counsel" results in tangible outcomes and impact that contribute to increased fundraising capacity and infrastructure. The "case" is one such example. Homework assignments and the prerequisites for fundraising success assessment are examples of two others. [1]

---

[1] A copy of the assessment tool is included at the end of this report.

Overview of Work With Participating Organizations

During 2014 Saad&Shaw worked with six nonprofit organizations at the request of The Assisi Foundation of Memphis, Inc. a mid-South philanthropic foundation. Those we worked with were:

Economic development and urban farming grassroots organization

15 HOURS | Creation of a case for support | Case complete: $64,300 raised in cash and in-kind support

Established performing arts organization

15 HOURS | Campaign readiness discussions, including guidelines for creating case and board workshop/engagement | Case created and workshops conducted; campaign committee formed; $1.3 million in gifts and pledges secured

Community development intermediary

20 HOURS | Creation of a case for support | Case complete: $30,000 secured for fundraising feasibility study and campaign plan

School-based tutoring program

5 HOURS | Assistance in making the case to expand program to more schools | Organization not ready to make changes that support increased fundraising

Health center

5 HOURS | Initial meeting held | Work to be continued in 2015

Community theatre

15 HOURS | Initial meetings focused on how to build fundraising capacity; current and mid-range strategies; and coaching for meeting with potential funder | Secured two-year $150,000 grant to support enhanced fundraising campaign; work continues in developing case

Case For Support
Economic Development And
Urban Farming Grassroots Organization

Saad&Shaw met five times with the husband-and-wife team who developed and have sustained this grassroots, community organization since 2008.

During the first meeting they shared their experience in developing and growing the multiple enterprises that comprise their organization. At the end of that meeting they decided to use our time together to develop a case for support for their urban gardening program, which is one aspect of their larger organization. We followed up with an outline that would guide the creation of the case.

We worked together for three months, during which they shared proposals they had previously written; answered specific questions we posed; and shared quantitative and qualitative information. We used content from their well-written proposals, repositioning the demographic, statistical, and financial information into more engaging tables and charts. We wrote up clarifying questions, shared via email, and discussed these during our one-hour in-person sessions. We used answers that were shared during these conversations to further refine the case for support.

Our hope was that they would have the case graphically produced using pro-bono services. While we felt this was an important goal, they were very pleased with the final document we presented without having it graphically produced, and they used it successfully to secure funds and in-kind resources.

Impact

The organization has raised $64,300 in cash and in-kind resources, including $3,000 from a crowd-sourced fundraising campaign, and $44,300 in cash funding. This includes a state grant of $39,500 which was an increase from the last grant of $17,500. The in-kind resources were for the major items they needed to expand operations, including a walk-in cooler freezer ($12,000 value), supplies for their aquaponics project, bees, and chickens.

Not The Right Time
School-Based Tutoring Program

Our work was originally to be focused on helping the organization create a case for support to expand its programming to more schools. They wanted to diversify funding by engaging major donors. Our first meeting was with the development director, and we reviewed and discussed the organization's current case and marketing materials.

Following that meeting, Saad&Shaw created two sets of questions for the development director and founder to review, discuss, and respond to. The first set was designed to guide our conversation with the founder and invited others; the second set was intended to inform work and discussion on a new case for support.

The second meeting was with the executive director, the development director, and the school coordinator. The founder did not participate. During that meeting the executive director spoke extensively of his assessment of the organization, its founder and board. He assessed the questions we raised as important, while simultaneously indicating that they would not be addressed, given the composition of the board and the current status of the organization.

Impact
There was greater acceptance of the organization's current status in the process of its development.

Board Involvement Established
Performing Arts Organization

The first meeting was with the development director and the managing director. Each took time to share their experiences with the organization, its productions, and the role of the board. They talked in detail about how the organization has faced its challenges and innovated programs in order to meet changing realities. They mentioned a "capital campaign" without providing detail regarding fundraising goals and priorities.

Very little time was allocated to sharing information about how we could be of service. As a follow-up, we sent them our Prerequisites for Fundraising Success assessment with a request that the organization's leadership complete the assessment and discuss their answers with each other. We posed specific questions related to the case for support for their proposed fundraising, such as the fundraising goal, use of funds, projected impact, and the extent to which "capital" needs were a part of their "capital" campaign.

During our second meeting the leadership agreed that facilitating two board workshops would be the most valuable use of our time. During both meetings the development director made it clear that he did not need help developing the case for support. Rather, the organization needed assistance securing board input and engagement. Staff wanted to secure participation from board members in a staff-led fundraising process.

We reported the organization's request to Dr. Young, and additional time was allocated. We prepared custom content for two workshops, with the majority of time allocated for small group work and discussion. Exercises were developed to encourage board members to take initiative in refining the organization's case for support (first workshop), and in role-playing gift solicitation meetings (second workshop). The workshops were both held in the Assisi Foundation's boardroom, and Dr. Young was able to observe and provide input.

We were stunned by the level of engagement at the first workshop. Board members actively participated, asking hard questions regarding their readiness and the quality of the draft case. They questioned each other and they questioned staff. The workshop ended with the development director saying he would revise the case according to their feedback and bring it to the next board meeting. The members responded with "no" — they wanted to update the case, and they would form a committee and meet within the next week.

Board Involvement Established
Performing Arts Organization

continued

At the second workshop, there was a revised case and a presentation by the vice chair regarding how the committee wanted to proceed with the campaign. At the second meeting, during the solicitation role-play exercises, the "potential donors" asked difficult and realistic questions of the "solicitors." We developed an evaluation form for board members to use to rate whether or not each solicitation role-play included 12 important elements of an "ask." We followed up with the development director with a suggested next steps document that provided guidance related to support and sustaining board leadership.

Impact

The organization has raised $700,000 in gifts and pledges and a $640,000 matching grant contingent upon its raising $2 million. "The campaign committee formed during our workshop sessions has been essential to the progress thus far." Average annual gifts by board members have increased from $1,500 to $10,000: these are in addition to campaign pledges.

Case For Support
Community Development Intermediary

Our initial meetings focused on the work of the organization, its success in attracting national funding, and the need to raise matching funds from individuals. We shared general information regarding successful fundraising, building diverse revenue streams, the process of engaging individual donors, and the need to engage board members in the fundraising process.

We asked specific questions related to fundraising, such as who the organization is seeking to raise money from, whether or not prospective donors and funders had been identified, how much had been raised to date, and whether or not the intermediary was competing against local economic development organizations.

We asked the executive to review and confirm the organization's mission and vision, and to consider how the organization could diversify its funding sources.

We crafted an outline of what the case for support should contain, and requested that he and his team begin compiling the requested information, inserting it directly into the outline.

Concurrent with our work, the president and his boards were developing their multi-year business plan and refining their marketing and communications messages. This increased the elapsed time of the project, as fundraising goals and projected use of funds were tied to the development of the business plan. We later learned that the questions we posed helped inform discussions and decisions as the business plan was created.

We compiled, organized, and edited information from the president and created a document with "suggested content" for the case for support. This document was provided to the organization's marketing firm with guidelines related to target audience and impact. The president simultaneously secured funding for feasibility interviews and the creation of a fundraising campaign plan. The marketing firm produced the draft case that was later tested in feasibility interviews.

Case For Support continued
Community Development Intermediary

Beyond The Grand Experiment, we interviewed 13 stakeholders to learn their response to the draft case for support. We presented our report to a meeting of the joint boards with a discussion focused on key findings, perceived strengths and challenges, and suggested next steps. We also facilitated a discussion about the extent to which the prerequisites for fundraising success were in place or in process.

In the next step, the case needs to be re-crafted to more clearly communicate the impact and use of funds that have already been raised, as well as proposed fundraising goals and projected impact.

Impact

$30,000 was raised to conduct fundraising feasibility interviews and create a multi-year fundraising plan. The board was exposed to fundraising prerequisites and questions raised within the philanthropic marketplace regarding fundraising priorities and use of funds.

Building A Fundraising Program
Health Center

An initial meeting was held with the medical director/executive director, chief operating officer, and the director of development. During this one-hour session the medical director/executive director discussed the health center's success in securing federal funds to build a new facility. In fact, the new building was almost complete when we first met, with the move-in scheduled for the following month. We agreed to meet again once the center had moved into the new facility and was operating well. The next meeting will occur in January 2015.

During a follow-up call the medical director/executive director and development director shared that they appreciated that we "stressed the importance of continuing with our fundraising efforts and not stopping where we are."

Impact
It is too early in the process to determine this.

5 hours

Strategy Development And Case
Community Theatre

The initial five hours allocated to this community theatre were allocated to discussions regarding how the organization could transform its capital campaign donors and season ticket holders into annual donors. We discussed the fundamentals of an annual campaign and the need to build the organization's fundraising capacity so it could become self-sustaining and able to fulfill its mission and vision, attracting the highest quality artistic talent.

Initial conversations covered the possibility of creating a signature event that would raise significant funds through multiple event-related revenue streams; strategies for making the organization a household name; the need for an annual campaign case for support, donor management software, and clearly defined roles and responsibilities; and a commitment to build toward a $1 million campaign over a multi-year period.

We also discussed the importance of donor stewardship and retention, and the consistency of donor attrition (20% to 30%, even with good stewardship). We provided detailed guidance regarding what to include in the case for support.

This organization used ideas and suggestions from our counselOnDEMAND sessions to craft a proposal to a local foundation. After the proposal was submitted, we worked with the executive, a staff person, and board member to prepare for a meeting with the funder's review committee. We challenged the numbers and assumptions built into the proposal, helping the organization prepare for the types of questions they might be asked.

Impact

The organization was awarded a two-year, $150,000 grant to cover staffing and other costs related to the launch of an enhanced annual campaign that targets donors who gave to its recent capital campaign, as well as season ticket holders.

Reflections

Built in success. The preconditions for success of this project were set by the organizations selected for an award. Dr. Jan Young of The Assisi Foundation of Memphis, Inc. held meetings with each of the organizations, "screening" them and selecting those who she believed could benefit from our special brand of fundraising counsel.

The nonprofit leaders we worked with demonstrated a high level of responsiveness and made our work together a priority. They kept scheduled meetings, completed "homework" assignments, asked meaningful questions, and in general were committed to and involved in the process.

Working directly with the executive director or board increases impact. Through our experience we have learned that fundraising must be a priority and focus of the executive director and board. If it is delegated to a development professional without the full commitment and engagement of the executive leadership and board, it is very hard for a fundraising campaign to be successful. The fact that we had the opportunity to work directly with the executive directors, and in one case the board, strongly impacted the success of the work.

The Grand Experiment is an ideal example of our motto, "start small ... plan BIG." Most organizations do not need to begin the process of building their fundraising capacity with a large investment in counsel. Starting small surfaces issues and "prerequisites" that need to be addressed prior to conducting a feasibility study, creating a campaign plan, or launching a fundraising campaign. Our experience has shown that applying a small amount of counsel can increase the effectiveness of subsequent larger investments.

Implied accountability increases impact. The fact that our work with these organizations was sponsored by a respected foundation as a "non-monetary technical assistance grant" had a great impact on engagement. First, the introduction by Dr. Young implied her belief in our work. This helped build the trust required for our work to be successful. Second, many of these non-monetary technical assistance grants were made in response to requests for campaign support or funding for campaign counsel.

Working with boards. The process reinforced our belief in our process for working with boards: you have to give board members something to respond to and engage with if you are to secure their involvement and leadership.

Three of the organizations accomplished more in 15 hours of time than other organizations have accomplished when engaging us for much longer periods.

Reflections *continued*

Case for support: more than marketing. We also learned the value and uniqueness of our expertise in the area of creating the case for support. During this engagement one of the organizations creating a case brochure chose to work with a marketing firm they had an existing relationship with. Our work with the nonprofit executive resulted in a document containing "suggested content for the case for support" and copywriting and design-related suggestions. Once the design firm began submitting drafts, we had to allocate a great deal of time trying to get the firm to modify the piece so that it would contain the elements our experience has shown us major donors and funders look for. The firm chose to craft a message that did not tie to the guidelines we had submitted. In the future, we will more strongly encourage organizations to let our copywriting and design team produce the case. We learned that we cannot assume a design firm has the fundraising-related knowledge and experience we have.

Affirming our expertise. Our experience includes working with nonprofit organizations and institutions across the country. We have worked with grassroots organizations, colleges, universities, hospital foundations, professional organizations, and organized philanthropy. Most have either been led by African Americans or serve predominantly African Americans or diverse communities of color. We have always felt that our tools and methodology are applicable to nonprofits in general, and The Grand Experiment provided us with an opportunity to work with an organization that had a predominantly white board and staff. We were personally gratified by the high level of engagement displayed by board members and the fact that they deeply engaged with the material and used it to organize themselves to raise money. The Grand Experiment demonstrated to us that our processes and work products are valuable and effective for diverse groups.

Building a culture of fundraising. The Grand Experiment has been a most positive experience for Saad&Shaw. It has introduced us to organizations and community leaders we might not have otherwise had the opportunity to work with. Our goal as a business is to prepare organizations for fundraising success. Organizations and institutions that are successful at fundraising often have a culture of fundraising that is generations deep. It is part of everything they do. One of our goals is to help emerging and under-resourced[2] organizations and institutions build a culture of fundraising. We seek to help them tell their story in a way that will attract funding. This is different from building a brand — it is about creating the case for financial support. What specifically are you seeking to accomplish and what will it cost? How are you using the resources available to you? We seek to help organizations identify the assets that are available within their network, and to build their network.

[2]"Under-resourced" is a relative term. It relates to the amount and quality of fundraising-related resources.

Reflections
continued

The Grand Experiment also reinforced a few of our prior learnings from the field. While these may appear simplistic, they have a profound impact on our work.

1. **You can't help people who don't want your help.** While it may be apparent to those outside an organization that fundraising counsel could be of great value, it won't be unless the leadership has also identified this need. There may be structural issues that inhibit successful fundraising as a priority. If an organization is not willing to address these, it will most likely continue to face challenges raising money.

2. **Sometimes we have to interrupt people.** In general terms we believe that listening is critically important to our ability to be of service to our clients. However, some people talk a lot and don't leave time for others to talk. This impacts their access to new information from others and can hamper the ability of other team members to contribute.

3. **We provide counsel.** We don't make decisions, and we can't make anybody do anything. Our goal is to facilitate an "aha" moment for the organizations we serve wherein they take ownership of ideas and find ways to bring them to life. We may believe an organization should do things differently, but they are the leaders of their organization. We are not all knowing — we have information and expertise to share that organizations can deploy within the context of their organizations, their communities, their leadership, and their history of successes and challenges.

4. **An organization's willingness to embrace fundraising is at the core of its ability to raise money.** "Needing" to raise money is not the same as having the willingness to do so. Despite great need, many organizations are unwilling to engage in the diverse activities that comprise fundraising. The majority of organizations participating in The Grand Experiment demonstrated a high level of willingness and attracted a corresponding high level of resources.

Growing The Grand Experiment

Reflecting on The Grand Experiment, we offer a few suggestions that could improve future engagements by The Assisi Foundation as well as by other foundations who want to help build nonprofit fundraising capacity. We suggest starting each engagement with an allocation of five hours to start, with the option (upon approval by the foundation executive) to increase to 15 hours or more (if needed) with commitment to an outcome. This could help participating organizations to focus on what they want to accomplish and to begin using the time most effectively from the very beginning.

This can be helpful for organizations that have multiple competing priorities. Once fundraising becomes a priority, the allocation of additional time can have more value than if the full award was granted without a personal understanding of the value of the time and its potential impact.

At the end of each engagement, participating organizations could be asked to write a one page report with quantitative and qualitative information. This could be completed in a Word document, or online using a tool such as SurveyMonkey.

The Grand Experiment could be of value to a larger number of nonprofits. It could be expanded in partnership with other local foundations. It could also be expanded to other geographic areas. While we have enjoyed the opportunity to work in-person with mid-South organizations, we have worked with organizations in other parts of the country and even with organizations out the United States, conducting counselOnDEMAND sessions by phone and/or Skype.

Questions could include:
1. Has this service impacted your organization? If yes, how?
2. What was the one thing suggested by Saad&Shaw that was most helpful to you?
3. What would you suggest could be done differently to increase the value of the engagement?
4. How would you quantify the impact of your work with Saad&Shaw? Examples:
   a. How much money has your organization raised as a result?
   b. Did your organization secure in-kind resources? If yes, which resources, and what is the financial value of those?
   c. Has board involvement changed? If yes, how has it changed?
   d. Has awareness of your organization increased? If yes, how has it increased?
5. Other comments.

Finally, as The Grand Experiment continues and matures, the foundation may want to establish optional criteria for participation. Having such criteria would allow the foundation to let the nonprofit community know that these non-monetary technical assistance grants are available and offer them the opportunity to apply. This could be a benefit to organizations that might not otherwise approach the foundation for funding or assistance.

Prerequisites Assessment

The following is a copy of the prerequisites assessment shared with participating organizations. This was used with the organizations' leadership to facilitate discussion during one-on-one working sessions. It was also used during one of the board workshops for the performing arts organization and during the presentation to the board of the community development intermediary.

Assess Your Fundraising Readiness

Take a moment to indicate your assessment of which prerequisites are currently "present," and which are "to be developed" at your nonprofit. Don't worry if you are "not sure" – simply indicate that as your assessment.

Present	To be Developed	No Sure	Prerequisites
			1. Attain full understanding and agreement regarding the organization's mission, vision, goals, strategic direction, and financial position amongst the organization's leadership.
			2. Achieve full commitment from the board of directors, CEO, executive director, or president, and top fundraising staff.
			3. Develop an active fundraising leadership team that meets regularly.
			4. Allocate funds and resources required for implementation of the fundraising plan.
			5. Create a clear, concise, and compelling case for financial support that ties back to the organization's strategic plan.
			6. Complete a fundraising assessment and feasibility study or survey.
			7. Develop a time-phased fundraising plan.
			8. Define roles and responsibilities for staff, board members, volunteers, and consultants.
			9. Hire professional staff whose primary role is fundraising management, volunteer training and management, and administrative support.
			10. Identify top-caliber volunteer leadership.
			11. Craft fundraising guidelines, policies, and procedures.
			12. Recruit a team of properly trained and informed volunteers.
			13. Use a donor database system to facilitate fundraising management and decision making.
			14. Coordinate solicitation strategies.
			15. Create a strong awareness and education program to complement and support fundraising activities.
			16. Thank and recognize donors and volunteers.
			17. Offer meaningful donor benefit packages and naming opportunities.
			18. Encourage open lines of communication amongst all parties, combined with a sense of urgency.

Start Small... Plan Big.

About counselOnDEMAND

counselOnDEMAND is a unique and affordable service introduced by Saad&Shaw in 2006. It is ideal for organizations who want to secure small amounts of fundraising counsel, and those with limited budgets. For some, it can be the first step in preparing for a feasibility study or creating a campaign plan. Others use it as an accountability tool to monitor monthly fundraising progress. The guidance we provide is tailored to each nonprofit's specific needs and requests. We work with organizations on projects such as:

1. Creating or strengthening a case for support, ensuring it is clear, concise, and compelling;

2. Building and sustaining a fund development team that engages board members, donors, and volunteers;

3. Engaging and supporting the work of the organization's board members;

4. Designing or enhancing donor benefits;

5. Identifying and engaging new potential donors or leadership-level fundraising volunteers;

6. Developing and launching home/office events and VIP tours that cultivate donors and encourage giving;

7. Designing campaign timelines and activity charts to guide the work of board members and volunteers;

8. Monitoring fundraising progress;

9. Reviewing funding proposals prior to submission to foundations, individuals, or corporations; and

10. Understanding and implementing the prerequisites for fundraising success.

About Saad&Shaw

Saad&Shaw provides clients with a unique brand of fundraising that combines marketing, corporate partnerships, and the best of business leadership with fundraising fundamentals. The firm works nationally and internationally and is known for designing innovative fundraising programs that increase revenue, strengthen partnerships, and provide value to all parties. Core services include campaign research, planning, design, implementation, coaching, and fundraising interventions. Clients include colleges and universities, health care institutions, grassroots groups, and philanthropy organizations.

The concepts and strategies employed by Saad&Shaw are based on the 60 years combined experience of principals Melvin and Pearl Shaw. Saad&Shaw are proud to offer one of the most experienced, innovative, and creative powerhouse partnerships in fundraising consultancy today.

Other Saad&Shaw Books

The Fundraiser's Guide to Soliciting Gifts: Turning Prospects into Donors

Have you been asked to raise money for a nonprofit, college, hospital, or church? Are you willing but not sure how to proceed? Is it your job to prepare volunteers and staff to solicit gifts? This book was written for you! You will learn:

1. Exactly how to ask for a gift to an organization or institution you believe in
2. What you need to know before you ask someone for a gift
3. How to close a meeting
4. How to follow up on solicitation meeting

Prerequisites for Fundraising Success: 18 Things Every Fundraising Professional, Board Member, or Volunteer Needs to Know

Want to jumpstart your fundraising but aren't sure where to begin? This book walks you through the steps for planning, launching, and maintaining successful nonprofit fundraising programs. Ideal for staff, volunteers, and board members at colleges and universities, philanthropies, health care institutions, and grassroots organizations. This user-friendly, workbook-style guide teaches the fundamentals needed to build a stronger organization and more secure financial future.

Both books are available through Amazon.com.

Learn More

To learn more about Saad&Shaw, including services, tips, and testimonials, visit www.saadandshaw.com.

Read Saad&Shaw's FUNdraising Good Times blog at www.FUNdraisingGoodTimes.com.

Meet the Authors

Melvin B. Shaw offers more than 45 years of experience in fund development and marketing. Formerly the vice president of marketing for the United Negro College Fund (UNCF), he created and produced the Lou Rawls Telethon, raising $4 million annually in corporate sponsorships and more than $500 million in annual gifts to date. Mel also served as the executive director of the Texas Association of Developing Colleges, facilitating joint programs and fundraising. He is nationally recognized for his work in creating and designing programs that combine marketing and fundraising and increase alumni/volunteer engagement. Mel's strategies create involvement and opportunities for corporate partnerships. He has developed cause marketing programs for Anheuser-Busch, General Motors, American Airlines, Chrysler Black Dealers Association, McDonald's, Essence Magazine, Disney World, and 7-Eleven.

Prior to forming Saad&Shaw Comprehensive Fund Development Services, he headed his own firm, Shaw & Company, which specialized in capital campaigns, annual giving, development assessments, feasibility studies, board development, campaign designs, and planning. Mel holds a Bachelor of Science degree from Lane College in Tennessee; a master's degree in business education from the University of Memphis; and was a fellow at Harvard University's Institute of Educational Management. In 1991 Mel received an honorary doctor of humanities degree from Lane College in recognition of his unique donor engagement and cause marketing programs and their impact on the fields of philanthropy and higher education.

Pearl D. Shaw, CFRE, is a fund development strategist and technical writer with management experience in the private and nonprofit sectors. Her private sector experience includes business development and marketing. Prior to forming Saad&Shaw Comprehensive Fund Development Services, she headed her own firm, Phrased Write, providing nonprofit organizations with proposal writing, executive coaching, and strategic fund development services including major gifts work. Proposals she wrote secured a combined $6 million for clients such as the Omega Boys Club, Regional Technical Training Center, Centro de Servicios, Bay Area Black United Fund, and American-Arab Anti-Discrimination Committee, San Francisco. As the principal writer for Saad&Shaw, Pearl writes the weekly column FUNdraising Good Times and is the co-author, with Melvin Shaw, of the books *The Fundraiser's Guide to Soliciting Gifts: Turning Prospects into Donors* (2012) and *Prerequisites for Fundraising Success: 18 Things Every Fundraising Professional, Board Member, or Volunteer Needs to Know* (2013).

Pearl served as a member of the board of directors of the Development Executives Roundtable from 2002 to 2008. She is a member of the marketing committee of the Women's Foundation for a Greater Memphis, and a member of the Association of Fundraising Professionals. She holds a Bachelor of Arts degree from the University of California at Berkeley, a master's degree in public administration from California State University East Bay, and is a certified fundraising executive. She was appointed to the board of Tennessee Lottery Corporation in 2014 by Governor Bill Haslam.

Made in the USA
Lexington, KY
05 June 2018